Intentions

Terri L. McCrea, M.Ed., LPC

Intentions

Cassaundra Mulligan, Editor

Cover and interior arrangements by
Kathrine Rend – Rend Graphics
www.rendgraphics.com

Printed in the United States of America.

ISBN-13: 978-1-7355737-4-8

Poetic Expressions by Terri
Terri L. McCrea, M.Ed., LPC, LPC/S
1643 B Savannah Highway, #113
Charleston, SC 29407
Mobile (843) 437-7572
Fax (843) 763-7202

Intentions

Dedication

This book is dedicated to those who dream but don't know how to speak their desires into existence. This book holds powerful proclamations of intentions for one's life. Utilizing the proclamations will add value, worth, purpose and joy into your world. Create a monthly, a yearly and five year personal and/or family vision board of intentions as you walk in your new beginnings.

No matter life's circumstances, don't let anything deter you from your renewed walk in your purpose, in your faith, with your passion and your renewed walk in grace.

Introduction

Today is the day to own an array of intentions to inspire one's walk towards one's purpose and towards one's destiny. Utilize this book's intentions or create your own intentions to help guide and motivate each step of your journey.

Reframing one's spirit from existing secretively, perplexingly, insensitively, heartlessly, frivolously, carelessly, judgmentally, sarcastically, dishonestly, passively, arrogantly, negatively, mindlessly, dangerously, nervously, selfishly, argumentatively, impulsively, angrily, worryingly, fearfully, impatiently or rudely doesn't occur overnight but it can be done with perseverance and commitment.

Retraining one's thoughts to live kindly, reliably, gracefully, patiently, tenaciously, lovingly. purposely, responsibly, joyfully, humbly, genuinely, honorably, virtuously, wisely, faithfully, passionately, peacefully, compassionately, adventurously, generously and thankfully is vital for intentional living.

Conceiving, believing and receiving the book's intentions will open you to a world of endless possibilities, heavenly living and a mindset that's free.

Today is the day to not only live free but more importantly, today is the day to live in peace.

Intentions

I intend on

using my story

to motivate,

to enlighten

and to inspire.

I intend on

blooming

the child within.

I intend on

walking in

my worth.

I intend on

cherishing

every second,

of every minute,

of every hour,

of everyday.

I intend on

embracing a

mindset of infinite

possibilities.

I intend on

freeing myself

from the

clutches of

slave mentalities.

I intend on

walking

faithfully.

I intend on

experiencing

life through

hopeful eyes.

I intend on

using my heart

as well as

my head

in matters of

love and life.

I intend on

being a

glow-getter.

The New Me

How I talk today will be different
in how I walk in truth tomorrow.
How I feel today will be different
in how I glow tomorrow.
How I exist today will be different
in how I passionately live tomorrow.
How I follow today will be different
in how I lead tomorrow.
What I held onto today
I will relinquish tomorrow.
What I dream today
will be my Deja vu tomorrow.
What was my crutch today
will be my platform tomorrow.

I intend on

turning my pain

into a passion.

I intend on

saving

me.

I intend on

walking

empowered.

I intend on

living

fearlessly.

I intend on

embracing

a life of

new beginnings.

I intend on

opening my heart

to true love.

I intend on

receiving

all of

life's blessings.

I intend on

defining friendship

based on empathy,

patience, reliability

and trust;

kind heartedness,

respect,

sincerity and

 unconditional love.

I intend on

forgiving

in order to live

abundantly.

I intend on

living

a heavenly

existence.

A Little Piece of Heaven

Sitting in quietness
at the week's end,
away from the world's angry chatter,
being moved by Caruso's Dalla,
soothed by Bach's Air on a G String,
captivated by Chopin's Nocturne in C
Sharp, transcended by Mozart's
Concerto for Clarinet,
inspired by Puccini's Nessun Dorma and
enveloped by Rachmaninoff's
Second Piano Concerto.

Heaven.

I intend on

living

boldly.

I intend on

living with

clear boundaries

to maintain

control

over my life.

I intend on

celebrating

my

existence.

I intend on

encouraging my

family to be the

best versions

of themselves.

I intend on

walking

my own path.

I intend on

living

without regret.

I intend on

growing through

self-reflection.

I intend on

doing

better.

I intend on

balancing

my mind,

my body

and

my soul.

I intend on

living a life of

serenity,

peace

and

tranquility.

When Stressed...

When stressed, you've got to...

Paint it out.
Walk it out.
Laugh it out.
Meditate it out.
Journal it out.
Think it out.
Color it out.
Talk it out.
Mantra it out.
Dance it out.
Massage it out.
Pray it out.
Read it out.
Swim it out.
Work it out.
Breathe it out.
Run it out.
Sleep it out.
Cry it out.
Yoga it out and
Sing it out.

I intend on

living

thankfully.

I intend on

nurturing

my temple with

self-love and

self-care.

I intend on

living

courageously.

I intend on

transforming

from a

swaddled cocoon

into a beautiful

butterfly.

I intend on

leaving

a

timeless legacy.

I intend on walking away from discounting, devaluing and disavowing relationships.

I intend on

eliminating

all the clutter

out of my life.

I intend on

living

self-sufficiently.

I intend on
assimilating
prayer,
meditation
and relaxation
into my life.

I intend on

preserving and

protecting

Mother Earth.

Mother Earth

She is fierce.
She cries.

She demands respect.
She is an old soul
with empath eyes.

She is temperamental.
She is rich.

She rests.
She is climactic.

She dods.
She joyfully sings.

She is organically perfect.
She is the impetus
for yearning wings.

She is patient.
She tenderly smiles.

She is timeless.
She tantrums
like an insolent child.

She births life.
She knows no fear.

She is not only
water and earth and fire,
but most importantly, she is air.

She beams with delight,
glowing in breathless sunsets and
shimmering in glorious sunrises.

She embodies the
aura of a gentle loon.

She is Mother
to those tender buds
that magically bloom.

She fights blind battles.
She is a majestic Queen.

She quenches droughts.
She is the rustle and sway
in vibrant autumn trees.

She is a gift.
She is hope.

She is unconditional.
She is an ethereal vision to behold.

I intend on

living

joyfully.

I intend on

paying

it forward.

I intend on

protecting

my aura.

I intend to

not only survive

but thrive.

I intend to

walk

with purpose.

I intend on

radiating

positivity.

I intend on

visualizing what

my fears

cannot see.

I intend to

walk with

clarity.

I intend on

living

debt, stress,

and baggage-free.

I intend on

living

selflessly.

Only Invite Those into Your World

I will only invite those into my world
who embodies love.
I will only invite those into my world
whose Visions soar higher than a mourning dove.

I will only invite those into my world
who not only support, but more importantly, respect,
understand and believe in my life calling,
journey and Dreams.
I will only invite those into my world
who empower me to be a better me.

I will only invite those into my world
who challenges sentences that end in but.
I will only invite those into my world
whose Heart has my heart's best interest at heart.

I will only invite those into my world
who can and will value a true friendship.
I will only invite those into my world
who I connect with on a Mental and Spiritual kinship.

I will only invite those into my world
who avows my king or queen-ness.
I will only invite those into my world
who honors my gifted genius.

I will only invite those into my world
who will impact mankind with their
magical purpose.
I will only invite those into my world
whose life's Mission is to
make a difference through
selfless service.

I intend on

spreading my

wings and fly.

I intend to

walk happy.

I intend on

living

virtuously.

I intend on

letting my

spirit light shine.

I intend to

grow

on my journey.

I intend on

living

authentically.

I intend on

living a

meaningful life.

I intend on

knowing that

"I can."

I intend on

embracing

my destiny.

I intend to

dream.

I intend on

living

graciously.

Don't Stop

Don't stop writing.
Don't stop growing.
Don't stop fighting.
Don't stop glowing.

Don't stop breathing.
Don't stop singing.
Don't stop healing.
Don't stop living.

Don't stop sharing.
Don't stop dancing.
Don't stop caring.
Don't stop laughing.

Don't stop creating.
Don't stop asserting.
Don't stop relating.
Don't stop exerting.

Don't stop dreaming.
Don't stop praying.
Don't stop believing.
Don't stop repaying.

Don't stop enacting.
Don't stop mothering.
Don't stop impacting.
Don't stop loving.

I intend on

speaking,

"I am enough"

into me.

I intend on

surpassing

my dreams.

I intend on

living

tenaciously.

I intend on

being an impetus

for the lost.

I intend on

cherishing each

gifted breath.

I intend on

being

a teacher

as well as

a student.

I intend on

dating me.

I intend on

living as

a caring soul.

I intend on

growing a

prosperous

business.

I intend on

embracing my

pricelessness.

Goodness

There is no

humanity,

compassion,

empathy,

virtue,

decency or

honor

being insensitive

to someone's pain.

Take a second, a minute or an hour

out of your day

to practice

goodness,

kindness,

mercy and grace.

I intend on
encouraging my
friends to be the
best version of
themselves.

I intend on traveling to all four corners of the world.

I intend on

getting into physical,

spiritual,

financial

and

emotional shape.

I intend on

raising my daughters

into virtuous,

capable

and strong queens.

I intend on

raising my sons

into honorable,

gracious

and merciful kings.

I intend on

embodying

the will of

my ancestors.

I intend on

seeing me

as

God sees me.

I intend on

awakening each day

to make

a difference.

I intend on

embodying

"I am."

I intend on

freeing

my mind,

my body

and my soul

of crippling

and exhausting

toxicity.

Seeds of Difference

I am a bloom from peace.
I am a bloom of kindness.
I am a bloom from humanity.
I am a bloom from color blindness.

I am an honorable king.
I am a regal queen.
I am a bloom of compassion.
I am a bloom of empathy.

I am defined through intention.
I am humbled through
mindful introspection.

I am a bloom of pureness.
I am a bloom from Mother Earth.
I am a bloom from rainbows.
I am a bloom from the spoken word.

I am an received conception.
I am a divine reflection.

I am a bloom from self-love.
I am a bloom that's risen above.
I am a bloom from the flames.
I am a bloom from the rain.

I am a bloom from life's inequities.
I am a bloom of resiliency.
I am a bloom of hope.
I am a seed of difference.

I intend on

embracing change.

I intend on

giving myself permission

to cry,

to feel,

to love and

to heal.

I intend on

growing

my kid's into

success stories.

I intend on

growing

as a person,

as a wife,

as a mother

and

in my faith.

I intend on

growing

as a person,

as a husband,

as a father and

as an

empathetic being.

I intend on

growing and

fostering

a mature

marriage.

I intend on

leaving

an everlasting impression

of my perseverance

and inner strength.

I intend on

surrounding myself

with souls

who embody the depth of

Mother Earth.

I intend on

living

intentionally.

I intend on

surrounding myself

with souls

who embody passion

like fire.

Survive

See you
through unconditional eyes,
while dreaming of better tomorrows
during quintessential nights.

Share your secrets
to quality living while planting
a legacy of hometown giving.

Never compromise
your value or your worth as you walk
healed of your wounds and repaired
from your brokenness.

Leave a path of glitter
wherever you go,
while empowering
encountered souls
to embrace their glow.

Be a warrior during
unprecedented vortices while
entrusting your higher self to direct
your metamorphosis.

Never concede, self-pity or
exhaust a good cry,
as you live with no regrets and
as you spread your wings and fly.

Stand like ancestors gone, while breathing in faith,
knowing you're never alone.

Embrace "I am"
like God's ever present clouds,
as you fight to survive while donning
that gifted crown.

I intend on

living

prayerfully.

I intend on

surrounding myself

with souls

whose energy

is calming

like cooling waters.

I intend on

embracing

my creativity.

I intend on

discovering

all sides of me.

I intend on

living

passionately.

I intend on

surrounding myself

with souls

who exude a gentle mood

like air.

I intend on

showing

that love

exists resoundingly.

I intend on

utilizing

my newfound voice

to state my truths.

I intend on

entrusting

my higher self

to direct

my metamorphosis.

I intend to

live

as a bloom

of resiliency.

Summary

When lost in translation about your past or when in doubt about your present or future, know that what truly matters is not your beginning, but the amazing chapters in between and it's beautiful ending.

Speak into existence not only your truths but more importantly your visions and your intentions, as you run fearlessly into the arms of your purpose, run courageously into the arms of your dreams and run boldly into the arms of your destiny.

Author

Terri McCrea is a native of Charleston, South Carolina. She has provided counseling for the past thirty-one years (twenty-three years of that in private practice). She graduated from St. Andrews Parish High School and the College of Charleston before receiving her Master's Degree in Clinical Counseling from The Citadel. She is an Adjunct Professor, a Licensed Addiction Counselor, a Licensed Professional Counselor, a Licensed Professional Counselor Supervisor and served as a Continuing Education provider for the South Carolina Board for Licensed Professional Counselors, Social Workers, Marital and Family Therapists, Psychologists and Psycho-educational Specialists. She conducts local and national workshops on her eighteen books as well as a Life Skills Summer Camp (ages five to eighteen), parenting classes, domestic violence classes and anger management classes. She is the Outreach Coordinator of the Old Bethel United Methodist Church's Community Outreach Program. This platform provides preventative, educational, rehabilitative, counseling, and evangelistic services to the Low Country's at-risk youths, families (including the elderly, poor, imprisoned, homeless, disabled and indigent).

Terri writes mental health articles for local magazines and newspapers. She guest appears for mental health segments on local radio and television networks. She conducts empowerment, intentions and leadership classes. She offers couples retreats. She can be described as a coach, counselor, visionary, poet, free spirit and believer that everyone and everything has a purpose. She is a member of the Poetry Society of South Carolina (PSSC), Old Bethel United Methodist Church Choir, Gamma Xi Omega Chapter of Alpha Kappa Alpha Sorority, Inc., the International African American Museum and is a proud aunt and grand aunt.

Terri is available for book signings, charity events, public/motivational speaking engagements, workshop facilitation, interviews, and expert appearances (radio, web, television and podcast) and poetry readings. She has self-published five self-help workbooks, four inspirational guides for couples in love, four empowering guides for tots/tweens/teens, a book of mantras and intentions, a book of wedding vows (English/Spanish translation), a how-to-date book and her first collection of poems (2007-2020).

Terri L. McCrea, M.Ed., LAC, LPC, LPC/S
1643-B Savannah Hwy, Suite 113,
Charleston, SC 29407
(main / principal) 843.437.7572
(facsimile / fax) 843.763.7202
poeticexpressions@att.net

*Visit/ visita: www.btol.com
                       www.Amazon.com
                       www.Alibris.com
                       www.Abebooks.com

Poetic Expressions by Terri Self-Published Books

- *The Power of Forgiveness: A Step by Step Guide on How to Let Go, Move On and Begin Living*

- *A Teacher's Dream: A Goal Setting Guide for Tots and Tweens*

- *Problem Solving One on One: Proactive Tactics for Millennium Youths*

- *Unleashing the Lion: A Parent's, Teacher's and Counselor's Guide in Understanding the Verbal and Nonverbal Language of Children, Tweens and Teens*

- *The Joy of Living: 20 Steps to a New Beginning*

- *The Joy of Living: Manifesting a Passionate, Purposeful and Positive You*

- *Unleashing the Lion: A Guide to Helping Parent's, Teacher's and Counselor's Understand the Verbal and Nonverbal Language of Children, Tweens, and Teens*

- *I Will Be…(Inspirational Quotes from Women of Faith, in Love and Standing in their Worth)*

- *I Will Be…(Inspirational Quotes from Men of Honor, in Love and Walking in their Purpose)*

- *It's Ok for Boys to…*

- *It's Ok for Girls to…*

- *Intentions*

- *Walk Like a King: 100 Virtues of a True Gentleman*

- *Elite Girls Wear Pearls: 100 Virtues of Strong, Empowered and Balanced Women*

- *The Book of Mantras: 100 Affirmations to Reframe your Thoughts and Retrain your Brain*

- *Soul Encounters: The Collective Poetry of Terri L. McCrea (2007-2020)*

- *Walking in Love: Wedding Vows for that Special Day*

- *2003. 2004, 2nd Edition 2008, What Price Are You Willing to Pay for Love? (Author house: ISBN: 1-418-6299-3 (e-book)/ISBN: 1-4184-3315-2 (Paperback)*

www.ingramcontent.com/pod-product-compliance
Lightning Source LLC
LaVergne TN
LVHW021353080426
835508LV00020B/2255